SAMMY SITSTILL

HOW SAMMY FEELS
ABOUT
ATTENTION DEFICIT DISORDER
AND
WHAT HE DOES ABOUT IT

Written and Illustrated by Dr. Catherine Thompson

Crescent Publications, Toronto, Ontario, Canada

SAMMY SITSTILL

HOW SAMMY FEELS
ABOUT
ATTENTION DEFICIT DISORDER
AND
WHAT HE DOES ABOUT IT

Dr. Catherine Thompson

Published by: Crescent Publications

Printed and bound in Canada

Canadian Cataloguing in Publication Data

Thompson, Catherine Margaret, 1946-
    Sammy Sitstill

Story in verse.
ISBN 0-9684750-0-0

1. Attention-deficit hyperactivity disorder–Juvenile poetry. I. Title.

PS8589.H4757S35 1999 jC811'.54 C99-930148-9
PZ8.3.T31956Sa 1999

Copies of the book may be ordered from the publisher:

CRESCENT PUBLICATIONS
31 Crescent Road,
Toronto, Ontario, Canada
M4W 1T4
(416) 413-1710

DEDICATION

SAMMY SITSTILL is dedicated to a little boy, James, and his family, all of whom are very dear to my heart. James' struggles to control his "beans" and the tireless efforts of his mom and dad and gran to support him have touched me greatly and were the inspiration for my writing this little book for other young children who experience difficulties controlling their attentions and high activity levels.

ACKNOWLEDGEMENTS

I am extremely grateful to a number of people who assisted in the production of SAMMY SITSTILL. It has been my habit for many years to begin each working day with two hours of reading and writing at the local donut shops and restaurants. SAMMY SITSTILL was conceived and written at the Belmont Restaurant. Thank you to Jim Anderson, a restaurant patron, for wondering aloud "what the heck" I was doing every morning and, when he found out, for connecting me to the helpful and friendly people at Image Plus Graphics. To Stephen Haddock, Jan Robertson, and Mike Osborn, your guidance and support has been an invaluable experience and is greatly appreciated.

To all those children with attentional difficulties who unabashedly and generously allowed me a glimpse into their inner lives, I thank them for giving me the opportunity to learn about and better understand their experiences.

And to Derek and Sean and close friends, whose loving encouragement prompted me to go forward with this book, thank you. Life just doesn't get any better than this!

Sammy Sitstill is not my real name
But it's Sammy Sitstill I am called just the same.
I hear "Sammy sit still!" so often each day,
That I've come to think of myself in that way.

There are beans in my stomach
That jump all around,

Throw me up in the air
And down to the ground.

They move this way and that
And that way and this,

That there's so much commotion
My seat I can miss.

The class laughs aloud
As they watch me fall down
And Miss Stern shows her biggest
And nastiest frown

And shouts "Sammy sit still
And listen to me.
If you don't pay attention
You'll stay in grade 3.

Stop horsing around
And stop being bad.
Sammy sit still
Or I'm going to get mad!"

I'm not trying to be bad
I say to myself,

But then I fall sideways
And knock down the shelf.

"Sammy sit still",
She says yet again.
"You're really becoming
Quite a huge pain."

I know I'm a pain,
I don't mean to be.
It's just so very hard
To be still when you're me.

I try to be quiet
But my voice pushes out

And Miss Stern gets all angry
And says in a shout,
"Sammy sit still
And be silent as well
And don't move an inch
Until you hear the bell."

But an inch isn't much
And the beans get their way,
So I have to stay in
At the end of the day.

Whenever I can't give
My best attention
Miss Stern makes me stay in
To have a detention.

Then she brings
The principal down
And Mr. Gooch too
Has a huge nasty frown.

He says "Sammy sit still,
Keep your feet on the floor.
Any more antics
And you won't see grade 4."

So I sit in my chair
And my skin gets all itchy
And my arms start to move
And my legs get all twitchy.

I look over here
And I look over there.
I can't look at one spot,
I look everywhere

And I wiggle
And giggle
And jiggle…

…and Mr. Gooch and Miss Stern both yell at me,

"Sammy go home!"

Some days I can't read,
Some days I'm a whiz.
It doesn't make sense
But that's how it is.

Sometimes I add well
And sometimes it's bad
And then the kids tease.
That makes me feel sad.

I run far too fast
All over the place
And Miss Stern yells,
"Sammy, you're quite a disgrace.
Sammy sit still,
Wipe that grin off your face!"

She says I have ants in my pants.
That's not true.
Miss Stern doesn't know
What I have to go through.

I make the kids laugh
But I don't see the fun.
When they see me come near
They all start to run.

They won't let me play ball
Or marbles or skate.
They say all I know
Is to make a mistake.

I want to play ball with the kids,
It's my dream,
But they won't let me be
A part of their team.

I say, "I run fast!"
They yell, "But you fall.
You can't hit a run
And you can't catch a ball."

I could do it, I thought,
If I really tried,
If only I could keep
Those beans quiet inside.

I sometimes get mad
At the drop of a hat
And have a big fit
And shout at the cat

And my mother gets tired
And says, "Sammy sit still.
You're giving me a headache
Your voice is so shrill."

So I try very hard
Not to let the beans out,
But the beans push so hard
They come out a big shout.

When I sit down to eat
–I'm often late–
I try hard to keep
All those things
On my plate,

But milk falls to the floor,
The peas on the table,
Though I try to keep order
As much as I'm able.

One day my mother said,
"Sammy my dear,
We need some assistance
It would appear."

So we went to a doctor
And I got quite a thrill
When he didn't scream "Quiet"
Or "Sammy sit still!"

The doctor said, "Sammy
I know what to do
To help you sit still
And stop feeling blue.

I'll help you to keep
From jumping around.
I'll help you to keep
Your feet on the ground.

Some children take pills,"
The nice doctor said,
"But Sammy let's first
Try this instead.

Because even with pills
There are things you must do
To keep those beans
From bothering you."

"You must eat your carrots
And spinach and beans
And broccoli and peas,
You know what that means.

All chocolate, candy,
And everything sweet
Will keep you from having
Control of your feet.

Eat bananas and apples
And pears every day
And I promise that you will feel
Better that way.

Don't eat ice cream
Or cheese or meat
And you'll find it much easier
To stay in your seat.

Water's your friend,
Eight glasses a day.
Drink it all up
And throw sodas away."

I tried to imagine
My life without sweets,
Instead eating spinach
And cabbage and beets

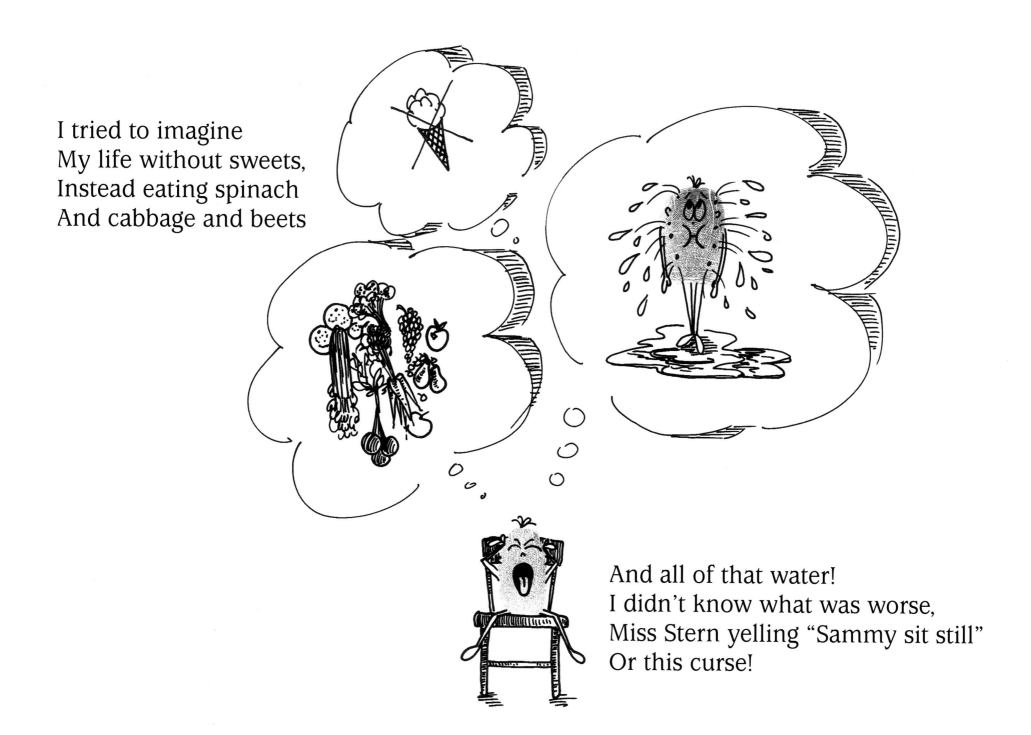

And all of that water!
I didn't know what was worse,
Miss Stern yelling "Sammy sit still"
Or this curse!

But then I remembered
All the times I felt sad,
When the beans bumped and jumped
And made everyone mad

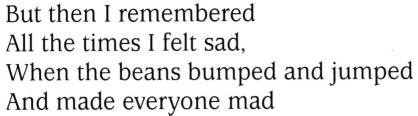

And the kids all laughed
And called me names
And wouldn't choose me
For any of their games.

So right then and there
I decided it was best
To do all I was told
To give these beans a nice rest.

The doctor said,
"This is important to do
Because the right kind of light
Helps children like you.

So go outside every day
And enjoy the sunshine
And run all around
It's going to be fine.

Do swimming, skating,
Cycling too
And make sure you're tired
Before you get through."

"Now homework is hard,
I see you agree!
But I promise it will be easier
If you listen to me.

Do school work in small bits,
Ten minutes at best,
Then move all around
And give your brain a good rest.

Then after you run
Sit down again
To do some hard work
For another ten."

"I know about beans,
I know how they jump
And force you to wiggle
And jiggle and bump.

So take a deep breath
Right up from the ground
And hold it in tight,
Let the air move around.

Then let it out slowly,
Don't be too fast.
It will make you feel calm
If you just let it last.

And then when you're finished,
Start over again
And again and again
Until you finish ten."

"Don't shout or hit
At your friends or the cat
Because if you do,
They won't like you for that.

If you work very hard
To breathe like I said,
Any angry thoughts
Will disappear from your head.

So what should you do
When you're feeling quite bad
And some of the kids
Make you get really mad?

HALT!

H means **HALT**, stop right there.
A is for **AIR**, breathe in the air.
L means **LISTEN** to what they have to say.
T is try to **TALK** in a quieter way."

"Now when you're at home
And you feel like a fight,
Go to your room
And with all of your might

Punch at your pillow,
Really hit it right smart
Until you feel better.
But that's just the start.

Then jump up and down
On a spot on the floor
Until you can jump
Up and down no more.

And rattle and shake
Your arms all around,
Try to shake out those beans
All over the ground."

"And when you no longer
Need to move and shout,
Sit down with your parents
And talk it all out."

"Take a nice warm bath
Before bed every night,
Then think a nice dream
And turn out the light.

If you remember
To do all that I say,
You'll feel a little bit
Better each day."

So I practiced to remember
All that he said
And got all those rules
Stuck well in my head.

The beans are still there,
That much is sure.
But the times that they wriggle
And jiggle are fewer.

And now that I'm learning
To hold my attention
I don't have to put up
With so much dissension.

But there's one more thing
That I'd like to mention…

...my name is Sammy Jones!

FOR THE ADULTS

If you have purchased this book, you possess or know of children who cannot focus their attention and/or control their high activity levels. Many of them will have received a diagnosis of Attention Deficit Disorder or Attention Deficit Hyperactivity Disorder. Have you ever wondered just how many times each day these children hear instructions such as –

Pay attention to me when I'm talking to you!
Be quiet!
Slow down!
Sit still and listen to me!
Stop fidgeting!
Stop bothering your classmates!
Play nicely!

For children with attentional difficulties, these and similar admonishments from the people in their world seem endless. And they're pretty pointless. Why? *Because they tell the children what must be done, but not how to go about doing it!* Consider, for example, how often we tell an overactive child to "Get control of yourself!". What does that mean to the child? Hold on tightly to yourself so you can't move? Or when we say "Pay attention to your work!", does that mean to look at it longer? Do these examples sound absurd? Imagine how confusing such instructions must seem to a child. And trust me, they hear them all the time.

Children with poor control over their attention and energy levels behave hastily and impulsively; their actions do not appear to be well thought out. Their behaviors tend to be disruptive to those around them. But they're not trying to be disruptive. They are merely doing what comes naturally to them. Something captures their attention and they go to it, without a thought that they're supposed to be focusing upon something else. Something within them makes them need to move about, so they move. They see something that they want right away, so they try to get it.

These children want to do what's expected of them, primarily because they'd like others to be pleased with them. But many of them lack the strategies for controlling the behaviors that others want them to control. Because they are frequently hearing statements of disapproval and displeasure regarding their behaviors, they begin to develop poor opinions of themselves and see themselves as failures.

Some ADD and ADHD children use medication. For some, it is necessary and it works. For some, it isn't effective. But even if medication is warranted, it is rarely the complete answer. Most physicians who prescribe drugs for these difficulties recommend that it not be administered in the evenings, on weekends, and during vacation times. What strategies are available to the children during these times? Medication alone, like our instructions, limit settings, and punishments, is something that is *done to children*. None of these tactics provide the children with the resources for *coping with their own behaviors.*

This is what Sammy Sitstill is all about. It's about teaching children how to take responsibility for themselves. Sammy tells a story about his thoughts, feelings, calamities, and social concerns in such a way that children can identify with him. There isn't anything that Sammy experiences that children with similar difficulties haven't experienced. Like all such children, Sammy tries very hard to do what is expected of him, but as he says –

> I know I'm a pain,
> I don't mean to be.
> It's just so very hard
> To be still when you're me.

Finally, Sammy meets with a doctor who tells him various things that he can do to help himself – safe, simple, healthy, and effective strategies that every child with attentional difficulties should know and can do on their own. Sammy clearly isn't fond of some of these strategies. But when he thinks back upon how his life is when he doesn't have control over his behaviors, he decides to give the doctor's advice a try. *It is vital that children possess their own resources for controlling their behaviors.* Other people repeatedly telling them what to do diminishes their self-images; knowing that they can control their own behaviors and taking responsibility improves their estimation of themselves.

This next point is extremely important. Because ADD and ADHD are diagnostic labels, they tend to be viewed as 'problems', as behaviors that should be eradicated. This is simply wrong! Having high activity levels and diverse attentions are only negative qualities when they interfere with the children's or others' ability to get something accomplished. There are many situations and settings where these qualities are positive and desirable. Creative ideas are not developed by individuals with overly focused attentions! Very high energy people frequently accomplish a great deal in their lives. Let's not attempt to completely squelch these qualities in our children. Instead, let's help them learn how to responsibly monitor their behaviors under a variety of different circumstances and situations.

Please read this book with your child – over and over and over again. It was purposely written in rhyme, since it has been demonstrated that a child's ability to recall information and instructions is enhanced with rhyme (can you remember learning the rule "i before e, except after c"?). With repeated exposure to the rhymed remedies in Sammy Sitstill, children will eventually find themselves thinking the remedy when problematic situations are encountered. Above all, have fun with your children in reciting and practicing these strategies together. Who knows – you may find that they're of some benefit to you as well!

2/00

Boston Public Library

The Date Due Card in the pocket in-
dicates the date on or before which
this book should be returned to the
Library.
Please do not remove cards from this
pocket.